IN HIS HANDS

Healing through Trauma and Trials

Lisa Parson

In His Hands
Copyright © 2024 Lisa Parson

ALL RIGHTS RESERVED. This book contains material protected under International and Federal Copyright Laws and Treaties. Any unauthorized reprint or use of this material is prohibited. No part of this book may be reproduced or transmitted in any form or by any means, electronic or mechanical, including photocopying, recording, or by any information storage and retrieval system, without express written permission from the author/publisher.

Unless otherwise noted all Scripture, quotations are taken from the New King James Version of the Bible. All rights reserved.

ISBN: 9798320203713

Produced by: Legacy Driven Consulting & Publishing

DEDICATION

This book is dedicated to my Children & Grandchildren. I also am personally dedicating it to my daughter who lived life with many generational curses and in return was killed by the sword. She was a beautiful soul, artist, and very loving. She opened her heart to those around her. She was so helpful to people and in return her kindness ended up taking her life. At the time of writing this book, her case is still unsolved. Going on four years our family has been seeking answers.

—In Loving Memory
Latisha D Nieto
1985-2020

Contents

DEDICATION iii

Chapter 1: The Beginning of Me 9

Chapter 2: The Beginning of the End 17

Chapter 3: The Nightmare of Trauma & Trials 23

Chapter 4: The Devil in Disguise 29

Chapter 5: The Escape 35

Chapter 6: Déjà Vu 39

Chapter 7: God's Love 49

REFERENCES & RESOURCES 55

Introduction

Who I Am

I'm writing this book about overcoming unforgiveness. I faced shame and rejection from going through physical and mental abuse, as well as being mistreated. Dealing with so much pain when I was young made me turn to addiction, and I found it hard to trust anyone, even myself sometimes. I hope my story of overcoming challenges will inspire those who read it, give hope to those who need it, and help people with unforgiveness in their hearts find a way to forgive. One important thing I learned during tough times was to find joy in them, no matter what, as James 1:2 says, "My brethren, count it all joy when you fall into various trials." We all face challenges, but it's how we handle them that matters. I pray that my story encourages you to persevere when faced with life's challenges and you receive the courage to walk in forgiveness.

CIERRA LA PUERTA

When I was five years old, I learned that some things happening at home had to be kept secret. It made it easy for alcohol and witchcraft to become a part of my life, and another side of me took over without me even realizing it. The Bible says, "Draw near to God and He will draw near to you. Cleanse your hands you sinners; and purify your hearts, you double minded." (James 4:8).

From the time I was five to fourteen, my parents were married, but my dad drank a lot, making him mean. I think his drinking problem started when he was a kid. My mom loved us, but because she went through a lot of abuse in her own life, she couldn't protect us. No matter where we were, if my dad was drinking, someone was likely to get hurt. I remember a camping trip when I was about thirteen. My dad, who was a member of the Knights of Columbus, got mad at me and my friends for taking a walk around the lake. I didn't even know we weren't allowed to go there. When we got back, I got punished; I got a beating. I stayed in my tent feeling embarrassed. I knew this wasn't the first time, and it wouldn't be the last. Abuse happens behind closed doors where nobody can see or hear. I grew up thinking, "What happens behind closed doors stays behind closed doors." This allowed another side of me to take over without me even realizing it. That's where my story begins.

Chapter 1

The Beginning of Me

I was born in August 1966 to a Hispanic family, and I believe I have a special purpose and destiny in life that was planned even before I was born. My parents followed different religions, and it made our family to be unequally yoked. My mom followed a religion called "The Truth." In their old church, they met in homes, and women had specific rules like not wearing pants, makeup, or jewelry. They also couldn't cut their hair or wear it down. People in this group only married within their community, so our family faced judgment because we weren't part of that community.

My dad, on the other hand, grew up in a Catholic family. In our Catholic home, we were taught to pray, take communion, and confess our sins to the priest (the father), who was like the head of the congregation. They taught us to honor our leaders, and in this case, the Pope was considered the most important leader in the Catholic faith. It was a bit challenging for us with two different religious backgrounds in our family.

Be sober; be vigilant; because your adversary the devil walks about like a roaring lion, seeking whom he may devour). **1 Peter 5:8**

FIRST SIGN OF REJECTION

After my mother got pregnant with me my father was stationed overseas so for the first few years of my life my family only consisted of my mother and her family. I spent a lot of my early ages while my dad was overseas spending time with my aunt and my cousins because my mom was always away. I was three years old when my dad came back from overseas and since I barely knew him, I was very skeptical about being around him at first. At times he would get upset if I didn't want to do something with him and I always wondered if that might be the reason, he soon rejected me.

I remember the abuse in my home starting when I was five years old. One night my parents were out of the house and my uncle came to the house to babysit and he did things that a babysitter should not be doing. The day after I had thought that God must've heard me crying and seen my tears because my parents found my underwear in their room, and they wanted to know why they were there and the truth. I answered and told them what had happened that night and the truth wasn't good enough for them. We went to go and confront my uncle who did this to me, and my mother didn't allow my dad to protect me in any way. My grandma gave me the worst look of disgust and made me feel as if it was my fault that it had happened to me. I didn't understand how someone could think like that when I was only five years old. How can someone so young be at fault for something so disgusting happening to them?

CULTURE AND TRADITIONS

Well remember I said I was from a Hispanic culture. Well things like this would get swept under the rug and forgotten, to be remembered no more. I never forgot because it never stopped. It continued for several years until I was a youth.

I was around eleven years old getting ready to go into middle school when I started taking my parents' cigarettes and getting into my dad's alcohol. I would take his alcohol from the home bar and later I started taking my friends prescribed medication to try and fill in the pain of abuse and rejection from my parents along with the sexual abuse I endured from my uncle. He had been molesting me every time he'd come around. I would try to hide from him, and I tried to convince my sister to go with him so that I wouldn't have to. I was so afraid of going with him because I knew that when I was with him exactly what he was going to do to me. I would just sit there crying afterward. I knew that I couldn't run anywhere. My parents would always want me to go with him even when I didn't want to, but us kids didn't have a voice, we were just told to do as we were told. No matter how uncomfortable it made us. You know that knot you get in your stomach like you want to throw up, the room starts spinning around, and all you want to do is run but you can't? That's the feeling I would get every time he would come around. All I could remember thinking to myself is that I was going to get through this. I was going to find a way out of this place someday. I had to learn how to deal with all the abuse at home and the abuse from my uncle because it was always swept under the rug and kept quiet.

My father was a horrible drunk. I remember that I was always the one that received a beating because I was the oldest and I was held responsible for anything my siblings did, even if it had nothing to do with me. I remember one time being beaten so badly that I peed myself, I had to change my pants and I had to get a wet towel and clean the wall because there was blood everywhere. This time, I was playing jacks outside on our driveway with my friend when my little brother came and kicked them all over. I pushed him and because of that I was beaten. I don't believe that I deserved that beating. That was the first time my dad had ever beaten me like that. I never hit or pushed my siblings again after that, I didn't steal, and I didn't lie. It didn't matter how much I told the truth, my family thought that I was a liar, because I was molested. At that point I started to feel ashamed, because my family knew the truth and they just couldn't live with themselves knowing that as the truth.

> The Bible says "The thief does not come except to steal, and to kill, and to destroy. I have come that they may have life, and that they may have it more abundantly." **John 10:10**

My parents ended up deciding to move and buy a new house because the area we lived in wasn't that great. There were always gunshots, gang fights, and rumbles. That's what they would call the fights on the school grounds. The school was right across the street from where we were living and I remember a bullet went straight through the window, through the closet, to the other side of the room. So, when we moved, I thought I would have a new life, a new start, a new school, and new friends. My first year in the sixth grade behind the barracks I was attacked by three boys. They raped me and I had no idea how I would tell my parents. It's not like they would believe me or care because at that point in my life I already knew that they never protected me. I ended up having the office call my aunt. I knew that my aunt sympathized with me and would understand how to support me. After this incident my aunt started taking me to church with her. Hanging out with my aunt was different from what I was used to.

I MET JESUS

I was thirteen when I met Jesus. I attended my aunt's church and there were people singing, dancing, and running to the front of the church. After church there would be a potluck. One Sunday I asked my aunt what they were all doing running to the front of the church she replied, **"They're receiving Jesus."** I then told my aunt that I wanted Jesus too, I wanted to be just like one of those beautiful women. So, I went up with everyone else and I received Jesus that day. I remember the women there wore long dresses that matched their shoes perfectly with matching hats. I loved the atmosphere at this church. I was going with my aunt until one day my dad told me that I wasn't allowed to go to church with my aunt anymore.

I BECAME A MESS

After my dad stopped me from going to church with my aunt. I started using alcohol and pills. This was my **gateway.** I had started practicing **witchcraft** more than ever and that's when my **second personality** really came out. I always had to be a different person at home than what I was outside the house. I remember around this time praying that my parents would just get a divorce because the abuse was being done to not only us kids but to my mother as well. Within the next year they started the process of getting a divorce. I never gave up hope through their marriage and in my early life that I would one day be free from the abuse.

Because my parents didn't trust me or believe what I said, I promised myself I'd trust and believe in my own kids. I taught them that I'd always believe them more than anyone else. So, when I read this part of the Bible about children having pure praise because they're innocent, it really resonated with me.

Do you hear what these are saying?" And Jesus said to them, "Yes. Have you never read, 'Out of the mouth of babes and nursing infants You have perfected praise'?" **Matthew 21:16**

Bible Verses for this Chapter of My Life:

<u>James 4:8</u> Draw near to God and He will draw near to you. Cleanse your hands you sinners; and purify your hearts, you double-minded.

<u>1 Peter 5:8</u> Be sober, be vigilant; because your adversary the devil walks about like a roaring lion, seeking whom he may devour.

<u>John 10:10</u> The thief does not come except to steal, and to kill, and to destroy. I have come that they may have life, and that they may have it more abundantly.

<u>Matthew 21:16</u> and said to Him, "Do you hear what these are saying?" And Jesus said to them, "Yes. Have you never read, 'Out of the mouth of babes and nursing infants You have perfected praise'?"

Chapter 2

The Beginning of the End

It is alarming to see that research shows that "23% of divorces are caused by domestic violence. Almost a quarter of survey respondents reported physical and emotional abuse in their marriages as a critical cause of divorce. Now before the age of 18, 85% of children will become victim to sexual abuse." (NCADV on reference page). "For the thief does not come except to steal, kill and destroy", John 10:10.

PHYSICAL & MENTAL ABUSE

My parents divorced and in the process we children were separated too. I didn't understand why they wanted us kids to be apart. However, I was glad when they finally divorced because I thought I was going to get a new start and a new life without abuse. I thought that I would finally have a voice and that my dad would listen to me since he never listened to me while he was married to my mom. They Never believed us kids. They always took what people told them as the truth. I wasn't ever allowed to do anything because I was always grounded. I was under the impression that

The Beginning of the End

maybe I was just a bad person. So, in return, I became this bad person that I was portrayed as. I started to be this bad person they always said I was, I started beating up other girls just for fun, I'd initiate them into my witch gang and make them do crazy things. By this time, I was already an alcoholic and learned about these cool pills that made you feel good so I was considered a pill popper. This was my gateway into the unknown. My second personality came out stronger because she was powerful. She saw what it looked like behind closed doors, she knew what it was to feel powerless.

Back to the divorce arrangements. My dad got my brother and myself while my mom got my two sisters. My dad moved in with his girlfriend at that time and they were never home. After a while of living with my dad and his girlfriend, due to the adults never being home, her son made his way into my room. He held me down and made me have sex with him. I couldn't scream because of how tightly he was holding me down. I was so scared of my dad and what he might've done if he had found out. I had no idea who I should go to in this time of need. I sat there crying wondering why I had been raped again. I ended up going to my aunt and my uncle's house and I had asked them to help me. They ended up calling my dad. Again, the whole time I was sitting there thinking to myself **"Is this my fault?"** My parents never believed me in cases like this. They weren't raising us kids the way God intended them to.

I reference this scripture below because I wanted to raise my children to go down a better path than what I was raised in and what God says here is saying that you are supposed to raise your children to seek what God has in store for them and not let them get pulled into the horrible things that the devil wants us to be pulled into.

> The bible says, "Train up a child in the way he should go {teaching him to seek God's wisdom and will for his abilities and talents}. Even when he is old he will not depart from it." **Proverbs 22:6 (AMP)**

THE TRAUMA KICKED IN

My parents only cared about their own selfish desires rather than the wellbeing of us kids. I later had to take a pregnancy test after being raped by my dad's girlfriend's son and when it came back positive, my parents made me get an abortion.

I remember the abortion very vividly because it haunted me for years. After being sedated the first time, I remember waking up in the middle of the procedure. I heard the vacuum noise, a sucking noise, and felt the tugging of the fetus all at the same time. I remember hearing the nurse tell the doctor **"She's awake"** and him directing her to put me back under sedation. I got stuck with an even bigger type of trauma from that moment forward. My parents refused to ever talk to me about this situation, they just swept it under the rug like they did when I was molested by my uncle. My dad ended up breaking up with his girlfriend and for whatever reason he was so angry at me.

THE BLACK OUT

My dad came to my grandmother's house after breaking up with his girlfriend and when he returned back to my grandmother's house, he started taking out his anger out on me by beating me horribly while he was drunk. The only thing that stopped him from beating me worse than he already did, was that my grandma threw herself on top of me to get him to stop. He then took me to my mother's house. While we were there, he didn't say a word the whole time. When my mother saw me, she took me straight to the hospital. I had three broken ribs, a broken nose, every blood vessel popped in both my eyes, and a fractured wrist. My clothes were still soiled from the beating. I was so scared I had peed on myself. I was only fifteen after that and I refused to talk to my dad for years. We were taught as children you never raise a hand to your parents or talk back, especially your dad. Besides, I was already afraid of my dad and the harm he could do.

> Fathers, do not provoke your children to anger, but bring them up in the discipline and instruction of the Lord. **Ephesians 6:4 (ESV)**

My dad ended up leaving my brother and I behind to move to California. I started to stay with my mother but she had a friend and her friends children, and my sisters living with her and I felt like I was intruding on their home life. Since I felt so out of place there, I didn't stay too long. Without my parents as a support system, it made life a little harder for me I feel. They wanted to have control over my life but they didn't want to be a part of my life and to me at fifteen and sixteen I couldn't understand why.

THROWN INTO THIS WORLD OF WOLVES

I ended up falling deeper into alcoholism, drugs, and witchcraft after this to try and fill the even heavier trauma I had just endured. I began doing séances, levitation, potions, and cursing people. I had been practicing since I was a young kid with my friends and my cousins. I was practicing white magic. They told me that white magic was better than black magic. At the time, I didn't know that magic was bad and that it was of the devil. I started practicing it with more mind control than before in hopes of hurting someone the way I was hurt by my family. We had been doing these things as kids playing Bloody Mary, doing blood covenants, trying to bring the dead back to life, putting spells on people, and going to grave sites to raise the dead. But as I got older and deeper into it with more mind control, I was so lost and confused during this time and ended up finding out that I was a witch. I was in a women's ministry meeting, testifying what God had did in my life. After the meeting one of the leaders approached me and explained to me that all magic was the same and it was all bad. I learnt from her that tarot cards, crystals, seances, ouija boards, conjuring up the dead were all evil practices. I did not know this, I believed it was normal because witch doctors were common in my culture.

Bible Verses for this chapter in my life:

Proverbs 22:6 Train up a child in the way he should go, and when he is old he will not depart from it.

John 10:10 The thief does not come except to steal, and to kill, and to destroy. I have come that they may have life, and that they may have it more abundantly.

Chapter 3

The Nightmare of Trauma & Trials

Will it ever end? Will it ever stop? Will I ever get through this? Will I ever get things right? Probably not. Why am I here? Why was I even born? These are questions I have asked myself over and over again as TRAUMA and TRIALS would come up and when we have been hurt at one time or another in our lives.

But this is where the Lord has led me and this is what the Lord says,

> "Listen, O coastlands, to me, and take heed, you peoples from afar! The LORD has called me from the womb; from the matrix of my mother, He has made mention of My name." **Isaiah 49:1**

WHERE DO I GO?

I met my first husband through a friend from school and we dated for a year and a half before I ended up pregnant at the age of sixteen. When my parents found out that I was pregnant by my boyfriend at the time, they immediately said that they wanted us to get married. We ended up getting married when I was five months pregnant. Even though we didn't want to get married. We did it for the sake of our families. I was forced to get married; I believed I ended up doing it to save my baby from being forced into another abortion.

ABANDONED

"When my father and my mother forsake me, Then the LORD will take care of me." **Psalm 27:10**

Our marriage didn't last very long, about five months. Because he ended up going back to Mexico where he was from because he couldn't handle life in the United States. Before I knew he went back to Mexico, (I actually thought that he was working in a different city) I was taking care of our daughter and working to be the mother I always wanted for myself. I had to grow up fairly quickly because there was nobody that was going to provide for my child the way that I was. I went back to school, got a job, and got on state assistance with the help of my aunt. A lot of people depend on the state to help raise their children and it becomes a thing that is passed down through generations. Especially when generational curses involve children at a young age. Along with depending on the state for help, many teenage parents are forced into being married, even if the people involved have no intentions of being in a committed relationship with each other. It's all a part of culture and curses that are passed down from generations.

CULTURE AND CURSES

Within the first year of my daughter's life, I was working and going to school. I eventually graduated from High School. When my daughter was six months old, I decided to go out and try to have some fun with some friends of mine. While I was out with friends that night, I ended up getting drunk and one thing led to another, and I ended up having a one-night stand. I was 17 when my oldest was born and 18, just graduating high school when my second daughter was born. Therefore, I was going through high school, working, taking care of my oldest.

Well, what was supposed to just be a one-night stand was more than I had bargained for. I was on birth control so I figured that much wouldn't come from it other than one drunk night. Later, I found out that I was pregnant. I told this guy that I slept with, who was an old friend of mine, and we decided that I would just go and get an abortion. When I got dropped off, I walked through a protest line while they tried to stop me from going inside. I went in and was sitting there in the office waiting for the doctor to come in after the consultation. This feeling came over me and I had remembered everything I had been blocking out from the trauma from years before when my parents made me have an abortion. How could I have forgotten that traumatizing event? It all came back like a flooding wave of flashbacks. I got so sick and dizzy, and I just ran out of that place and never looked back. I ended up having my second daughter months later, her father and I decided we were better off friends rather than lovers. Until, I realized we couldn't be friends either. I couldn't trust him watching my girls because while I was at work, I would have neighbors calling me saying that he was leaving my kids alone. I had a hard time being able to trust anyone with my daughters because I had a rough upbringing, and I didn't want anything to happen to my kids.

In the time that he was a part of my life, I had him babysitting my kids and found out later he was abusing my daughters, which I found out from taking my youngest daughter to the doctor and she refused to let the doctor see under her diaper. When I tried to leave him, he said that if he couldn't have me or my kids then nobody could. He became very possessive, and I thought I was going crazy one night because my oldest daughter started throwing her doll in the corner saying, "Bad Baby." At that moment, I didn't know what else to do. I ended up going to the hospital down the road and telling them that I thought I was going crazy. I wanted to hurt this man who was hurting my babies. I finally was able to talk to someone who in return ended up helping me more than I could imagine. She helped me get a car and an apartment. I started living my life the best way I could and trying to provide for my daughters and myself.

A TEMPORARY HOME

Not too long after I ended up getting my daughters taken away from me. My mother believed that I was not fit to be a mother to my kids. I did everything I could to get them back. I slept in my car outside the house where they were and continued to go to work. I ended up just living with my mother temporarily while still proving to the state that I could care for my kids and working.

The event leading up to the removal of my kids from my care was due to my baby's dad leaving them alone while I was at work. I approached my boss to tell him that I had been called by a neighbor that my kids were left alone. I told him that I had to leave, and I went and picked the children up and brought them to my job. I let my manager know that I was unable to finish my duties. Then my baby's dad and the police showed up at my job and stripped me of my children and took them to Children Protective Services. I then went and asked my mom for help because I didn't know what else to do to try and get my children back. So, I stayed temporarily with her until I could get the help and assistance, I needed to get them back.

At this time, I ended up meeting a nice man who made it seem like he was going to take care of me and my daughters. I remember thinking this man was the man of my dreams. He said he served in the army; he had a car, and he was a manager at his job.

I remember thinking to myself, "WOW! I finally will have someone who will be there for me and my kids who truly wants to be there." At this time, I was still living with my mother trying to find a place of my own and he was living with his parents. It took me from going to my mother for help until I was back on my feet for me to finally do what I needed to as a mother for my children. I had to promise my mother that I wouldn't talk to the father of my daughter because he was causing so many issues for me in order for my mother to even help me. It worked though, I got what I needed in order to be back on my feet and take care of my kids. I even fell in love with someone who was willing to help me with my children along with working and being there for me and my kids. Or so I thought…. I got put into the system. I kept my job, got my own apartment, sought counseling, got state assistance and state childcare. It all worked and benefitted me and my children.

Bible Verses for this Chapter of My Life:

Psalm 27:10 "When my father and my mother forsake me, Then the LORD will take care of me."

Chapter 4

The Devil in Disguise

No matter what I do, will it ever get better? I'm going to church, homeschooling my children to protect them, but am I really protecting them or harming them? Is there really a God out there? I keep hearing about him. These were the questions that I would recall and go over them in my mind. I started trusting in God and believing that God fights your battles with you. My grandma always told me "Don't lose your faith in Jesus" I began seeking a church and started finding out who this Jesus was. This scripture is the one I was led to when I needed to be shown that God was fighting these battles with me, and I truly wasn't alone.

"For though we walk in the flesh, we do not war according to the flesh. For the weapons of our warfare are not carnal but mighty in God for pulling down strongholds, casting down arguments and every high thing that exalts itself against the knowledge of God, bringing every thought into captivity to the obedience of Christ, and being ready to punish all disobedience when your obedience is fulfilled." **2 Corinthians 10: 3-6**

THE SECOND HUSBAND

When I met this man, he claimed to be such a great guy. He had a job, had a military background, a car and most importantly he wanted to care for me and my daughters. We ended up getting married and living together. By the age of twenty, I had been in my second marriage and had three kids. I ended up being initiated into this man's family gang by his sister. Soon after we were married, I would become his punching bag because he was jealous of my girls because they weren't his. I couldn't take it so every time I would try to defend my girls, he would turn on me and we would fight. Later in our marriage we ended up getting custody of his older son who was four at the time. Just eleven months older than my oldest daughter. I ended up raising four children from that moment forward. No matter how much I tried to protect my children from him, I couldn't. He started abusing them while I was at work. I had to work two to three jobs at times and put myself through college, while in this marriage because he started refusing to work himself.

THE ADDICT

> "Be sober, be vigilant; because your adversary the devil, as a roaring lion, walketh about, seeking whom he may devour". **1 Peter 5:8**

I found out that my husband was cooking drugs, a drug addict, an alcoholic, and he was using me as a mule and a cleaner. It was such a dangerous life for me and my children. I saw so many things when he had me as a distributor to the jail and a cleaner. I was anxious after seeing a place blow up, it kept me being on guard all the time for what was going on all around us. During this time, I was forced to start using crank (Crystal Meth, it's street name when it first came out was crank) with him while I was working his little business and trying to take care of my kids. For thirteen years I was married to this man who was not only abusing me, but my kids. I grew tired of the lifestyle he had us living together. One of the times he was arrested, when he got out, he told me that he was changed. He said he found God and was going to church, so we started going to church together but it didn't last long before he started doing the same stuff as before. The kids and I kept going to church even though he wasn't. It kept us away from home longer and away from him. I worked at the church, for school lunches, and my regular job. After work I would pick up my children and we would go to the movies or the mountains. There were times that we would just drive around because I didn't want to go home to fight.

I grew weary of coming up with reasons for the bruises and the shame, all because he acted just like my dad did back then. He would hit me even in front of others, like that one time when my best friend was there. He had been hitting my kids, and when I witnessed it, I didn't hesitate—I immediately called the cops. But he got furious and punched me in the eye. My eye swelled up, I had visible marks, and my kids were crying. My friend saw the entire incident, but she was so scared that we just left without knowing what to do.

I BECAME SUICIDAL

Amidst all the stress and abuse, there were moments when the urge to just drive my car into a brick wall overwhelmed me, a desperate attempt to escape it all. At times, I resorted to taking pills, but nothing seemed to bring relief. I even ended up in the hospital after experimenting with drugs. I found myself transformed into a mother raising kids, a struggling drug addict, a functioning alcoholic, and a victim of domestic abuse. It was as if the generational curses from my family's past were finding their way into my own life.

In the midst of this turmoil, I kept attending church, and through baptism, I and my kids found a renewed faith. It marked the beginning of my plan to break free from the cycle of abuse. It took a total of five years to carefully plan my escape. Along the way, I had to file for bankruptcy, and unexpectedly, we moved in with my grandfather, this was not a part of my original plan.

> "I can do all things through Christ who strengthens me." **Philippians 4:13**

But my grandfather grew ill and requested that I move in to take care of him. Since I had been going on the weekends to clean his house and help in the garden, and nobody else wanted to take care of him, he asked me to. Since I was the only one who was there for him when he needed someone, he left me an inheritance, his house.

One day, when I was taking my two oldest kids to Middle School, I came back home, and my youngest son looked upset. I asked him why, and he told me he was tired of his dad hitting his sister. I went into the room to check, and sadly, it was true. She had been beaten because she didn't get her stepdad coffee.

I got really angry. I walked out of the room and heard him yelling at my sick grandfather. I went up to my husband and told him not to speak to my grandfather that way. He pushed me. I told him to leave, but he didn't like that. He started choking me, and my two children were there yelling at him to let me go. He then went after them. I grabbed a salt shaker and threw it at him. After that, I told my kids to run and lock themselves in the bathroom. He got mad, started choking me again, so I grabbed a pan that broke while trying to get away. I saw another pan on the wall, so I took it to protect myself. All I could think about was how many times I asked him not to hit me and my kids, and to make me go where I didn't want to go. I blacked out, and all I saw was the blood gushing out of his head. I almost got charged with attempted murder if God hadn't been with me that day.

Bible Verses for this Chapter of My Life:

<u>1 Peter 5:8</u> "Be sober, be vigilant; because your adversary the devil, as a roaring lion, walketh about, seeking whom he may devour."

<u>Phil 4:13</u> "I can do all things through Christ who strengthens me."

<u>2 Corinthians 10:3-6</u> "For though we walk in the flesh, we do not war according to the flesh. For the weapons of our warfare are not carnal but mighty in God for pulling down strongholds, casting down arguments and every high thing that exalts itself against the knowledge of God, bringing every thought into captivity to the obedience of Christ, and being ready to punish all disobedience when your obedience is fulfilled."

Chapter 5

The Escape

Taking care of business, going through the escape process, going through treatment, filing for a divorce, caring for my grandfather, and saving my four children from abuse was coming to an end. I was leaving everything I knew behind and moving forward. Psalms 23:1-3 says, "**The Lord is my shepherd; I shall not want. He makes me to lie down in green pastures; He leads me beside the still waters. He restores my soul; He leads me in the paths of righteousness For His name's sake.**" I had so many fears for what life was going to bring my way, but I had to go on for my children's sake. I had to show them that life was going to throw trials in life that everyone was going to face several times throughout life. There were going to be good and bad times in life but they must continue to go forward and never give up in life. I taught my children how to survive, how to recognize pedophiles, I taught them the importance of education, and to trust nobody. I had no idea that they were being touched within the home. The oldest son I had, that we adopted, had issues that were handed down and I wasn't aware of them until later in life. I thought I had saved my children from any kind of sexual abuse, but the sickness was still there within my walls. My children had been damaged and I was the one at fault. I couldn't save them from molestation within the home, I couldn't save them from the physical abuse.

HOW DID I LET THIS HAPPEN

I shared before that my ex-husband got custody of his oldest son when he was just four years old, and he was already hurt. I put him in therapy, counseling, and speech therapy. I had to stop his dad from hurting him several times, choking him for things, especially after his mom passed away. I became his adopted mom to protect him and raised him as my own. However, he faced more abuse from his stepdad, my husband. I had four children to care for and protect.

I had to close my home care business and switch from a full-time to a part-time job to look after my grandpa, who was getting sicker. We made important decisions, created his living will, and he chose to die naturally, without more meds or insulin. The doctors gave him three weeks to live. His kids didn't like that he left everything to me, but I was only following his wishes. I went to school to learn about caring for a diabetic naturally, and he lived two extra years.

Before my grandpa passed, he mentioned never having a Christmas, so I planned the best one ever. We got a tree with lots of lights, and he smiled at it. He allowed us to have a dog. I went through surgery because of cancer in my uterus. Something went wrong during the procedure, and I almost died. I continued drinking and went back to work. Then, I met my future husband while caring for my grandfather and kids. I dated a guy who had been in prison and ended up back there on a parole violation. Later, my grandfather passed away, and I inherited the house and some money.

THE INHERITANCE

> "The Lord is my Shepherd I shall not want." **Psalm 23:1**

I continued to live life with just me and my children. We laid my grandfather to rest at the military cemetery. I was still healing from the divorce, the surgery where I almost died, and now burying my grandfather, who felt like a dad to me. He was the last family I had left besides my kids. The sadness from losing my brother came back, and all the grief hit me at once. I wondered where my kids would be without me. The fear of almost dying and not knowing where my kids would end up scared me because I had no family, and I didn't know if they did either. Except for each other. I always told my kids, "You guys are all you have in this world," because that was true in my life.

I had hidden my second personality so well that nobody knew about it for a very long time. Nobody could tell the difference between the two. The guy I was seeing asked me to marry him over the phone while he was in prison. When he got out a few years later, we had a zoot suit wedding with lowrider cars, my dream wedding. This was my third marriage and the one that felt like a true dream come true. God finally led me to a man I would love, and who would take care of me.

Bible Verses for this Chapter of My Life:

Psalms 23:1-3 "The Lord is my shepherd; I shall not want. He makes me to lie down in green pastures; He leads me beside the still waters. He restores my soul; He leads me in the paths of righteousness for His name's sake."

Psalm 23:1 "The Lord is my Shepherd I shall not want."

Chapter 6

Déjà Vu

Now, my children are all grown up and have their own families, facing challenges I never wanted them to experience. It's like adding a chain link from the dysfunctional family we were raised in—no communication, love, feelings, or compassion. These are just a few things we go through, but the Lord says in **Hebrews 13:5-6,**

> "Let your conduct be without covetousness; be content with such things as you have, for He Himself has said, 'I will never leave you nor forsake you.' So we may boldly say, 'The Lord is my helper, I will not fear. What can man do to me?'"

GENERATIONAL CURSE

While I was dating my husband and later married him, my kids started graduating one by one. When I was married, I had my two youngest still living at home and they were having trouble in school and in relationships, just like their mother. One of my daughters got the worst of the abuse from my ex-husband and was also being molested by her step-brother and I didn't find out until it was too late. She was out of control just like I was, she was violent with everyone especially me and at the time I didn't understand why. She was going down the same path I did, but I didn't even see it even though I tried to show them, I was actually blinded to the truth of what was going on in the house. She ended up with two children that I later ended up with custody, because she was only fourteen when she ran away and got pregnant the first time and within two years she had her second baby. One day she came, and it was very obvious that she had a drug habit that I didn't know about right away.

I was just trying to keep her away from this older boy that took her innocence away and now she was just like me. We ended up getting into a domestic dispute and I ended up in jail and on probation and she took her daughters back. These poor girls went back and forth between me and my husband, to their dads' parents, and then to their parents in between. Shortly after my husband's daughter came into our lives and added an addition to our family. She didn't respect me and she tried everything to separate my husband and I to the point she accused me of abusing her. I had to go through an intense investigation that I had never gone through before. I spoke out that she had been through a lot of neglect throughout her life and abandonment issues with her mother passing away and her dad being in prison all her life. When she got her life together all she wanted was her daddy all to herself, but with her wrongfully accusing me of abuse, I had to have her sent to a group home where my friend was a coordinator so they could get us family counseling to see if that would help readjust us to live together.

It didn't work like it was supposed to. The family took her out and to this day, she's still one of our lost children, homeless, on drugs, and living the criminal life in and out of jail. My other children have been here and there over the years. Some don't communicate with me because of the abuse they endured and the witchcraft that was instilled upon them at a young age by myself.

> Behold, I give you the authority to trample on serpents and scorpions, and over all the power of the enemy; and nothing shall by any means hurt you. **Luke 10:19**

After a few years I had reverted back into drugs with my husband and his brother. I found myself following right behind them thinking I was going to save my husband because I became his drug dealer first. Then, I started using it when it got out of control. There were many nights that I would spend alone because I would give my husband ultimatums, either me or the drug and he always chose the drugs. So, in time I started to partake in these drugs with him. We were using crack cocaine and at the time the only other drug I had ever dealt with was crank which was a completely different drug. It lasted a total of four years with my husband and two years with myself. I was an Assistant Manager moving up to become a General Manager in a restaurant inside a Casino when, my husband reverted back into drugs after being clean for a while and he had managed to hide it from me for two years. He was telling people to break into my house and steal so that he could get his fix, and he was forging checks in my name and cashing them. I didn't know that I had married an ex-con, a criminal. It got to the point where an investigator was hunting him down. I had to give my husband a choice, me or the drug and since he chose the drugs again, we separated for a while. I was tired of begging him to come back home when he just kept choosing the drugs. When he finally decided to come home, it was hard for me because there was no trust at that point. He had broken all the trust I had in him because of all the things he did while he was using drugs. I ended up quitting my job and lost it all within a short amount of time. I lost everything: my kids, my house, and most of all my life. I didn't have anything anymore. I resorted to my last and only option and I called my mother pleading for help.

We needed to get out of this state, so I called my mother and asked her to help us out. We ended up leaving the state to go get the help I needed to save my husband. When we attempted to drive out of the state, my car broke down, and so we ended up having to ask my mother to fly us out to her. Drugs was just everywhere, and it was to the point where we didn't even have to buy it anymore. We had hit rock bottom together. We spent a month in Pennsylvania with my mother and her husband in this small little country town where he was a Pastor of this little country church. We attended with my parents so that we could get clean and then return back home. The first thing we did was go and get our fix. While we were in Pennsylvania my husband was making money so, all that we could think about was going back and getting high. Instead, we came back with a change of mind and heart. After we got high that time, we came back feeling so guilty about it.

JESUS SAVED MY LIFE

My sister invited us to her church, and we started going there every day, even if it was just to sit outside the doors. We needed to be away from home. After attending for a few months, we were invited to an event called Harvest Fest. They did an altar call, and I could feel a tugging at my soul that wouldn't go away. I didn't really want to get up and go anywhere, but my spirit kept telling me to go. Eventually, my spirit won, and I went up to the front and rededicated my life to the Lord.

It was just the beginning. That night, I went home and was literally delivered from all my demons. Everything that was anti-Christ in my life up to that moment came out of me like a demon. The Lord allowed me to witness what He pulled out of me, or more like vomited out of me. It may sound crazy, but a four-legged creature with a furry head and body and red eyes came out of me. God showed me all my sins, and it's a struggle to let it all go. God made it clear that from that moment on, I needed to remain in the light.

Déjà Vu

"You are the light of the world. A city that is set on a hill cannot be hidden. Nor do they light a lamp and put it under a basket, but on a lampstand, and it gives light to all who are in the house. **Matthew 5:14**

I woke up my husband because I was freaking out, but all he could see was the fear on my face. He didn't see what I did. I didn't want the lights off because that thing kept trying to get back inside of me. I was able to see it in dark places, under the cabinets and in the dark places of the house. My husband and I just prayed and the next morning I got down on my knees at the edge of my bed and I prayed again. About three days later we went to church and this man that we didn't really know came up to us. He said he had a dream that God spoke to him that he was to give us a place to live, and we were to leave our house and everything in it, not take anything out of it, and to give my husband a job. I almost fell over because just three days prior, I had prayed that if we weren't meant to be in our home, to remove us, and God removed us. We continued to go to church there, my husband worked, we went to Bible study, and attended the addiction ministry. After a couple of years, we got custody of our two oldest granddaughters. After getting custody of our granddaughters, we continued to attend church, seek spiritual guidance, and trust in the Lord's plan for our lives.

I FELL AGAIN

I was doing a women's brunch Bible study on the weekends that was really going well, or so I thought until one day my husband disappeared. I already knew the signs when he didn't come home. I started to notice some of the signs that my husband was using again. All he would say when I caught him was "I brought you some." I couldn't believe that after all that God had done to get us away from drugs, he would go back to it and even bring some home to share with me. All I could do was cry and fight the urge for as long as possible. I prayed and prayed to get it out of our lives, but then we met people in the church who did it also. The devil used people in the church to make us backslide right back into it. We continued to go to church and attend the addiction ministry there, and I kept praying that God would remove the drug dealers from my husband's life because that was our weakness. One by one, the dealers started to disappear.

Not very long after, I found out that I had cancer again, and I started to worry. Why me? It felt like it was one thing after another. I had been feeling sick for a while after we had moved, and I thought it was just the withdrawals or maybe it was menopause. It had to be one of these, I thought. So, I started taking natural vitamins, but what I was taking ended up making it worse; it was feeding the cancer all along. I truly didn't care about myself, but I had responsibilities, so I went to the doctors and they found large lumps in my breast and started sending me to more and more doctors. It all went by so fast; I was sitting there, and the first

Déjà Vu

results had come back as stage 3B cancer, which would later be stage 4 as the cancer had spread to the other side and possibly my kidney. My first thought was I'm going to die. I began to cry, and after this diagnosis, I told my husband just to take me to my friends, and he did, and he got me what I wanted. I went home and tried to commit suicide. I thought if I was going to die anyway by having cancer, then I might as well just die right then and there. While I was sitting there crying and asking God why me, why do I always have the raw end of the deal, why am I still here, why...isn't this working? When all of a sudden, I heard **GOD'S VOICE** say **"BECAUSE YOU'RE NOT GOING TO DIE, I'M NOT DONE WITH YOU YET."**

> I shall not die, but live, and declare the works of the LORD. **Psalm 118:17**

From that moment, my husband turned to me with tears in his eyes and said, "I don't want you to die." I then began to tell him that God spoke to me and said that I wasn't going to die and that He wasn't done with me. We both sat there crying and held each other closely. From that moment, my husband did a complete 180-degree turnaround. He has been a changed man from that day forward. A couple of days later, we went back to the doctor, and while we were sitting there, I heard **God's voice** again say, **"Now, go and get anointed by your head pastor, for he will have a word for you."** Of course, I went directly to the church from there. We got prayed over, anointed, and given a word by our pastor. At our next doctor's visit, they mentioned I needed chemo right away, but first, I had some business to take care of. I had to say goodbye to my family, so we sent my granddaughters to Pennsylvania with my sister and met them there later. I just had to make sure all my medical stuff was taken care of first. When we returned from Pennsylvania, the cancer treatment would begin.

Déjà Vu

Bible Verses for this Chapter of My Life:

<u>Hebrews 13:5 NKJV</u> Let your conduct be without covetousness; be content with such things as you have, for He Himself has said, " I will never leave you nor forsake you. So we may boldly say. "The Lord is my helper, I will not fear. What can man do to me?"

<u>Luke 10:19 NKJV</u> Behold, I give you the authority to trample on serpents and scorpions, and over all the power of the enemy; and nothing shall by any means hurt you.

Chapter 7

God's Love

Dear Heavenly Father,

May this testimony glorify You in every way. May it touch the hearts of those struggling with unforgiveness and addiction. Let them know, Father, that You are their saving grace. Show Yourself to those who lack faith because of their situations, whether it be family, abuse, or alcoholism. Thank You, God, for saving me and always showing up when I least expected.

> "Who bore witness to the word of God and to the testimony of Jesus Christ, to all things that I saw."
> **Revelation 1:2**

WALKING BY FAITH AND NOT BY SIGHT

Being diagnosed with breast cancer and going through treatments was hard. My body was refusing it at first. My hair started falling out, so we decided to cut it short, and then my husband shaved my head and his. This was a hard thing to do, taking three hours, as I had never shaved my head before. After chemo treatments, it was

God's Love

hard to eat anything but sherbet and broth. Solid foods became impossible. I started losing my fingernails, my hair, my skin turned ash gray, and I got sores from the chemo. I caught pneumonia and almost died. Rushed to the hospital, another time I needed a blood transfusion, and all I could do was pray. Pray that God would get me through, pray that my husband would find strength in God if I died, and pray that my children would return to my life.

Then came radiation, a year later, and after that, I got reconstruction on my breasts. Years of treatment and healing led to a diagnosis of PTSD. I filed for disability due to the trauma, but God was on my side. We moved into a rent-to-own house and our church community supported us during this time. They sat with me during chemo, brought meals, and cleaned my house.

NEW LESSONS TO LEARN

I thought I was healed after cancer. I was going to Zumba and would feel like a champ. However, I realized I had to change my lifestyle. I had to learn to live with new changes. Reading books and researching, the list began: no stress, no sugar, no caffeine, etc. I had to cut people out of my life due to stress. I let go of generational curses, knowing God gave us authority to cast out demons.

"And when He had called His twelve disciples to Him, He gave them power over unclean spirits, to cast them out, and to heal all kinds of sickness and all kinds of disease." **Matthew 10:1**

After the cancer journey, I continued raising my granddaughters. One day, I received a call that no mother wanted to receive. My daughter had been shot, and I needed to call the hospital. It was too late, and the last time I saw her was at the viewing. She left three children behind, and her murder remains unsolved.

GRIEVING AND COVID

Expect the unexpected through prayer and fasting. God answers prayers through obedience, prayer, and steadfastness. I received an unexpected apology from my uncle, for abusing me as a child. I believe it was only God's work. Many people never receive an apology to bring closure to this episode in their life. I am grateful to God for hearing my cries.

Every day, I ask God to help me forgive the people who hurt my daughter, even though it's been four years. Father God showed me they were just tools of the enemy. He also showed me my daughter was meant to be here for a reason, planned by Him even before she was born. This helps me forgive them. If I love God and want forgiveness, I must forgive too, because He forgave me first. So, I pray every day for them to find salvation and repentance, just like

I prayed for years for my uncle to own up to what he did.

COVID was a season of mourning. I lost my daughter, I was grieving, I felt alone and isolated in this pain. Four years later, things are getting better. I found a new church, and life's looking normal again. However, I still faced some tough times—sickness, losing my home during the pandemic, caring for my uncle with dementia and Parkinson's disease. Even when things get tough, we must keep hope, stay strong, forgive ourselves and others, and follow God's teachings. That's how I got through all the tough stuff.

I learned forgiving myself was key before I could forgive others. When I saw Jesus' love in myself, others could too. We need to trust in Jesus because He keeps us steady, like an anchor. That hope we have in Him keeps us strong, even when things are hard. (Hebrews 6:19)

LEARNING THE NEW ME

Don't lose sleep, and don't lose hope. God answers prayers in His timing. Overcoming trauma and trials with forgiveness and faith is possible. I am thankful for Father God, I hold my head high and continue to heal.

> "Have I not commanded you? Be strong and of good courage; do not be afraid, nor dismayed, for the LORD your GOD is with you wherever you go."
> **Joshua 1:9**

> "Do not be afraid or discouraged, for the LORD will personally go ahead of you. He will be with you; he will neither fail you nor abandon you"
> **Deuteronomy 31:8 (NLT)**

The Lord will stand by your side forever as long as you open up your heart to him. He will carry you in his hands while he guides you down the path to righteousness.

> "Don't you realize that you become the slave of whatever you choose to obey? You can be a slave to sin, which leads to death, or you can choose to obey God, which leads to righteous living." **Romans 6:16 (NLT)**

Thank you, Lord, for working in my life and allowing me to share my story, in hopes of inspiring others.

In Jesus's name, Amen!

Bible Verses for this Chapter of My Life:

Matthew 10:1 "And He called to Him His twelve disciples and gave them authority over unclean spirits, to cast them out, and to heal every disease and every affliction."

Joshua 1:9 "Have I not commanded you? Be strong and of good courage; do not be afraid, nor dismayed, for the LORD your GOD is with you wherever you go."

Revelation 1:2 "Who bore witness to the word of God and to the testimony of Jesus Christ, to all things that I saw."

REFERENCES & RESOURCES

- NCADV National Coalition Against Domestic Violence The Hotline.org 1-800-799-SAFE (7233)
- U-Turn For Christ
- www.uturnforchrist.com
- About.com Alcoholism Turquoise Lodge of Albuquerque NM Substance Abuse Services
- http://alcolholism.about.com/od/tx_nm/index.htm
- http://alcolholism.about.com/library/blupdate.htm
- Women's battered shelter private information
- http;//www.breakingcycle.org
- Sageclinic.org Mental & Behavioral Health
- The Family Connection LLC www.TFC.health
- American Cancer Society
- http://www.cancer.org
- Relay for Life Los Lunas
- www.relayforlife.org/loslunasnm
- Cancer Support Now
- www.cancersupportnow.org
- Toll FREE (statewide) 855-955-3500
- Albuquerque 505-255-0405
- Jesus is my Anchor Ministry Support Group
- Jesusismyanchor6.19@gmail.com 505-503-4447
- THE BIBLE – New King James & Amplified Versions

Made in the USA
Columbia, SC
18 August 2024